MEDIEVAL LIVES

Merchant

ROBERT HULL

W
FRANKLIN WATTS
LONDON•SYDNEY

First published in 2008 by Franklin Watts

Copyright © Franklin Watts 2008
Artwork copyright © Gillian Clements 2008

Franklin Watts
338 Euston Road
London NW1 3BH

Franklin Watts Australia
Level 17/207 Kent Street
Sydney, NSW 2000

A CIP catalogue record for this book is available
from the British Library.

Dewey number: 940.1

ISBN 978 0 7496 7739 8

Printed in China

Franklin Watts is a division of Hachette Children's
Books, an Hachette Livre UK company.

Artwork: Gillian Clements
Editor: Sarah Ridley
Editor in chief: John C. Miles
Designer: Simon Borrough
Art director: Jonathan Hair
Picture research: Diana Morris

Picture credits:
Bibliothèque Mazarine, Paris/Archives Charmet/Bridgeman Art Library: 16. Bibliothèque Municipale, Valenciennes / Alfredo Dagli
Orti /The Art Archive: 10. Bibliothèque Nationale, Paris/Flammarion/Bridgeman Art Library: 11. Bibliothèque Universitaire de
Mèdecine, Montpellier/Gianni Dagli Orti/The Art Archive: 40. British Library, London/The Art Archive: front cover, 23, 32, 37.
British Library Board, London, All Rights Reserved/Bridgeman Art Library: 29. British Library, London/HIP/Topfoto: 9b, 14, 17, 21,
27, 30, 36, 39tl, 39tr. Castello di Issogne Valle d'Aosta/Giraudon/Bridgeman Art Library: 38. Collegio del Cambio, Perugia/Gianni
Dagli Orti/The Art Archive: 5, 9t. Koninklijk Museum voor Schone Kunsten, Antwerp/Bridgeman Art Library: 20.
Museo de Arte Antiga, Lisbon/Gianni Dagli Orti/the Art Archive: 33. Musée Condé, Chantilly/Giraudon/Bridgeman Art Library: 41.
Museo Correr, Venice/Alfredo Dagli Orti/The Art Archive: 28. Osterreichische Nationalbibliothek, Vienna/Alinari/Bridgeman Art
Library: 24. 35.m Palazzo Medici-Riccardi, Florence/Bridgeman Art Library: 8bl, 19. Palazzo Pubblico, Siena/ Alfredo Dagli Orti/The
Art Archive: 13. Private Collection/Bridgeman Art Library: 25. Charles Walker/Topfoto: 15t.

Every attempt has been made to clear copyright. Should there be any inadvertent omission please apply to the publisher for rectification.

CONTENTS

Introduction   8

First days   10

House and home   12

Growing up   14

School   16

Becoming a merchant   18

Marriage   20

The wool trade   22

Travel and communication   24

War and piracy   26

Secrets of success   28

Branching out   30

Wealth and property   32

Merchant's wife   34

Good works   36

Health and diet   38

The end   40

Glossary   42

Timeline/Useful websites   43

Index   44

INTRODUCTION

The medieval period of European history runs from about 1000 to about 1500. It was a time of momentous events. In 1066 England was conquered by the Norman French king, William the Conqueror, and his nobles. During most of the 14th century, France and England fought a series of wars called the Hundred Years War. In addition, Christian crusaders fought with Muslim Arab armies over the control of Jerusalem. When the Black Death, or plague, struck in 1348, it killed around one-third of the population of Europe, altering the balance of society.

Feudal society

At the beginning of this period European society was thoroughly 'feudal'. Kings owned all the land, but a class of knights was granted land in return for service in war. Knights made similar arrangements with holders of manorial estates, and they in turn with those below them. This went on down to the peasants, who were granted a few acres of land to farm, to which they were 'tied', in return for fees and heavy service obligations. This network of agreements held society together.

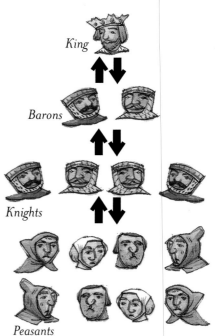

A network of services and obligations held feudal society together. Merchants, however, were outside this structure.

King

Barons

Knights

Peasants

Safe, walled towns such as this were good for trade.

A merchant writes a letter, while an assistant stands by.

Throughout the medieval period, great building projects went on – of monasteries and abbeys, houses, colleges, castles, churches and cathedrals.

Towns and trade

Especially from the 13th century onwards, there was a rapid development of trade. Society became less feudal, as rents paid as money took the place of many services. Money payments also took over from exchange, or payments 'in kind'. The ability to buy things with money spread to all groups except the poorest. Gradually many peasants became more free from feudal services and fees. They bought land, became artisans – skilled workers – and moved to towns.

Towns grew in number and size, led by a prosperous class of burgesses, merchants who made their living in national and international trade. Certain features that became modern banking techniques began to develop, particularly in Italy, where banks agreed to treat as equivalent to silver or gold a piece of paper with a promise to pay, the forerunner of the cheque.

Farming

But the medieval world was still an agricultural world. Most people worked on the land, to feed themselves. They would take any surplus produce to market, and with the money they earned buy household items such as garden tools, pottery or clothes that they did not make themselves. They might buy these from travelling salesmen, 'chapmen'.

The wool merchant

The export of wool from England, Spain and northern Africa to the weaving looms of Italy and Flanders was one of the great trading phenomena of medieval times. Merchants in England made fortunes from buying wool produced in wool-growing districts and selling it to cloth-merchants from Europe.

This is the story of a typical medieval figure, who was born into a family of shopkeepers but who became a prosperous merchant.

Chaucer

The poet Geoffrey Chaucer had first-hand knowledge of the world of merchants; his father was a vintner (wine merchant), and some close friends were merchants. 'The Prologue' to *The Canterbury Tales* has a vivid sketch of a merchant with:

❖ *...a forked beard* [dressed] *in mottelee.* [And] *...high on horse he sat; Upon his head a Flaundrish beaver hat...*
– a high horse and an expensive hat from Flanders. He speaks *...ful solempnely* – rather pompously– and talks non-stop about the money he's making: *Sownynge alway th'encrees of his wynnyng...* Chaucer makes the very words whine. He clearly doesn't like this merchant!

A wealthy merchant on his horse.

FIRST DAYS

The woman has worked downstairs in the family shop during her pregnancy. She has come up to the bedroom to give birth, helped by a midwife and women neighbours. The women wash the newborn boy carefully with warm water, and rub him down gently with a mixture of roses and salt. A finger dipped in honey is rubbed in his mouth. They wrap him in 'swaddling' clothes, long strips of cloth, as they believe this will help his limbs grow straight.

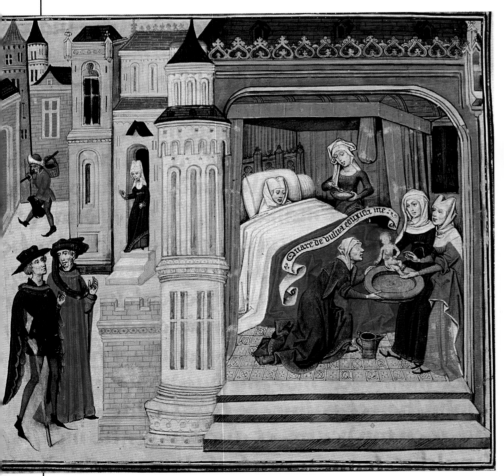

Female servants and relatives see to the washing of the new baby, as richly dressed visitors approach the house.

Baptism

Baptism into the Church comes next in his life. This baby is healthy, but if he had not been, the midwife would have performed the actions of baptising him, as she has been taught to do. It would be done quickly because the priest's and the Church's teaching is that a child who dies unbaptised will not go to Heaven.

Being healthy though, he is taken to the church, with as many family and friends as can be there – and perhaps not his mother; and he is baptised at the big stone font. The priest speaks the words that bring him into the lifelong care of the Church, and sprinkles holy water on him. One of the three godparents names him.

Medieval facts

The figures relating to the mortality of medieval royal babies, children and young people make sad reading. Royal babies and children had the best care available then, but of the approximately 96 children born to the kings and queens of England between 1150 and 1500, about 34 died in their first year, and a further 22 died before they were 20. And the figure of 96 does not include stillborn children, or those who died at birth. Plague and war caused a handful of the deaths.

The husband accompanies his wife to the 'churching' ceremony.

When the mother is strong enough to go out, she is 'churched', at a service of purification; the Church believes that giving birth, being fleshly and unspiritual, is a contaminating process.

Sleep and nourishment

The baby's food is his mother's milk until he's nearly three. He doesn't drink cow's milk or water because they are not really safe. The solid food he has is chewed for him, or 'strained', in his mother's mouth first.

The baby sleeps in a cradle. When he is older, his mother will let him share a bed with his brothers and sister. When he is weaned (no longer breast-fed), he will sit at the table to eat. His father and mother use wooden armchairs; the children sit on stools. They all wear hats, to help keep warm, even at the table.

The older children get clouted gently when they behave badly at the table. Their parents repeat what the books about children's table manners say: don't wipe your nose on the tablecloth, don't wriggle, don't gulp your food.

Medieval facts

In some parts of Europe it was believed that fireflies were the souls of unbaptised babies.

Medieval facts

The mothers of babies who fell ill often tried 'religious' or superstitious remedies. One was to measure carefully the sick child's body-height, and present a candle of the same height as an offering at a shrine. Or sick children might be taken to a saint's tomb, and laid there for a while. In another case, a baker from Canterbury borrowed a garment that was supposed to have saint's blood on it, washed it in water, and gave the water to his son to drink. The boy recovered.

HOUSE AND HOME

The downstairs part of the young boy's house is a shop, where his father and mother sell hats and caps, and various other things like thread and ribbon, beads and cheap ornaments, and even paper and some board-games. It is open-fronted, but at night his parents close a shutter over the counter.

A group of shops, with outside stall-like counters and living quarters over the shop.

following guild rules, an apprentice sleeps at night. Steep stairs lead up to a small first-floor living area and bedroom.

During the day, the child wanders round the shop and back room, watched by his mother, playing there while she shows goods to possible customers, or sews things for sale, or sees to the cooking or other household tasks.

Living in a shop

Behind the shop area is another room, reaching up two storeys to roof height. There is a fire here, to warm the house and for cooking; the smoke wanders up into the roof-space and out under the tiles or through the window opening.

The room is also a storage-place and a workshop for making things they sell. There are benches and stools, a trestle table for display, a board with counters for making calculations, ladders to reach the shelves and cupboards, and in the corner is a small bed where,

Town houses

This house is one of the first in the town to be built in a row of three, with another shop next door. This new arrangement makes building cheaper, but if a fire breaks out in one wooden house it will spread to the others quickly; fires devastate whole areas of towns, even destroy them. So the new town regulations ensure this house has a roof of slates, not thatch.

In front of the shop is a noisy, dirty street. It is, though, less cluttered than it used to be, and cleaner. There are new regulations against leaving piles of timber or heaps of manure in the street, or digging holes in it. They help the shop's trade.

Dirt and refuse

The town has men to carry refuse away, to empty and replace the backyard midden and the cess-pit that collects waste from the indoor 'privy' or lavatory. The street is still smelly, but it used to be worse. Not even the worst smells wake up sleeping toddlers. Noise, though, does, and the street is very noisy. Horses and carts pass through all day long, traders call out non-stop, there's a continuous din from the cook-shop next door, the forge and the carpenters' shops further on, and from the tavern and market stalls. When all that quietens down, there are still the church bells. The toddler can pop his head out at the front for a while, as long as someone's

keeping an eye on him. His mother takes him to the market stalls with her, too. He starts to see the town.

The evidence suggests that medieval town houses were of varying construction and size, from simple two-room dwellings to splendid town houses with separate kitchens and stables surrounding courtyards, and gardens beyond. Archaeological evidence survives — wood and stone, seeds in cess-pits, and so on — and in some places whole buildings still stand, usually altered or added to. This evidence needs careful interpretation and sometimes it is difficult to be sure what people did in these buildings, or who they were.

A street in Siena, as painted in about 1340, showing pack-horses, sheep and merchants trading, with glimpses of indoor scenes, including a teacher at a desk.

GROWING UP

After the shop is closed up, there is still work to do. But there is entertainment as well by the fireside, telling stories, or playing board-games.

A man and a woman pass the time with a board-game.

Wandering the town

There are no parks, but the young boy has the town to wander in. He can throw sticks in the stream, build little dams there, catch stickleback. He can play with a ball in the street, walk along walls or climb piles of wood.

He is free to roam these streets near home, but animals use them too, and there is always danger: from horses' hooves and cows' horns and the teeth of pigs who shouldn't be there but who have escaped their pens. There are risks from being too adventurous as well. Youngsters have drowned in millponds and from falling off bridges into the river.

Games

There are games to play with friends, brothers and sisters: hide-and-seek, tag and hobbyhorse. As he grows older, he joins with the grown-ups in various boisterous sports: football, cockfighting, wrestling, archery, and even pretend battles with lances. In winter, young and old skate and play games together on the ice.

There are other entertainments too that appeal to the growing boy, such as plays performed by members of craftmen's guilds that retell stories from the Bible.

Fairs

There is a market in the town and sometimes a fair, with travelling entertainers to watch, like *gestours*, who perform story-poems with great bravura and gesturing, and jugglers and minstrels, and *podicicinists*, or wind-breakers, an entertainment his parents frown on.

A group playing cards.

Another entertainment parents frown on is the habit boys have on winter festival days of going round the town dressed up, singing songs and asking for money or food. It's fun for boys though.

Some other kinds of fun are seasonal, like autumnal scrumping – stealing fruit off trees – playing football with the bladders of newly-slaughtered pigs in November and, of course, snowball fights in winter.

SCHOOL

One medieval teaching book asks grimly: ❖ *Are you willing to be flogged while you learn?* ❖
Schools could be dangerous for teachers, too. John the Scot, the story goes, was killed by his pupils at Malmesbury, with their pens.

The boy's parents know that, if he is to succeed in trade, their son must learn to read and write. When they signed the agreement for their oldest son to become an apprentice, the master craftsman promised to teach him reading, writing and grammar. Their daughter is beginning to learn her alphabet too, taught at home by her mother. Their younger son needs to go to school.

A schoolmaster – in this case a monk – and a group of pupils, from a manuscript.

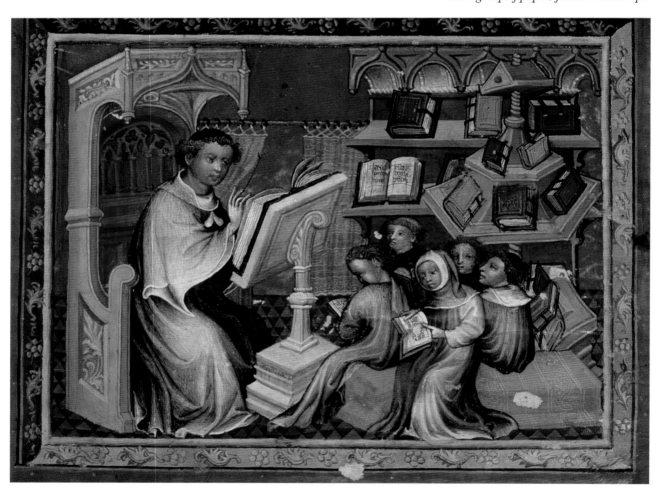

Going to school

There is a small boys' school in the town, taught by a schoolmaster in his own house. Early every morning the shopkeeper's son puts on his stockings, shoes, robe and belt; he collects his 'penner' – a sheaf for quills – and his knife and horn tube containing ink, and sticks them in his belt. He takes his own candle because it will be dark in the schoolroom, and runs off through the cold streets to be there by seven o'clock, and pay the fee. He will be at school all day, until late afternoon, though he will have two long hour-or-more breaks, one at about ten o'clock and another at lunchtime.

The boys learn their alphabets, and begin to learn by heart then read aloud 'The Lord's Prayer', 'The Ten Commandments' and other religious extracts. They read from a much-fingered, greasy 'primer', which is a book written out by hand, by the schoolmaster or perhaps by a monk from the nearby monastery.

Reading

The boy 'reads' at first by rote – from memory – without understanding. It is boring, but he tries hard because if he makes mistakes he is likely to get beaten. He is lucky that he is learning his own language first, rather than Latin, as children once did. Later he will learn to read some Latin too, including verse by heart, and a book of grammar.

He learns to write by scratching his letters on a waxed tablet. Occasionally he uses ink on scraps of parchment. He learns to count, using counters placed on a cloth with lines marking columns for units, tens, hundreds and so on. He has to calculate answers to simple questions of arithmetic.

A teacher of geometry with instruments and shapes.

Corporal punishment

A commonplace medieval notion was that corporal punishment was necessary, 'a good thing'. A 14th-century French manual for monks teaching in a Dijon song school – where boy choristers learnt to sing church services and received education – has these grim lines:

❖ *At Nocturne, or any of the Hours, if the boys commit any fault in the Psalmody or other singing, either by falling asleep or by other transgressions, let there be no sort of delay, but let them be stripped forthwith and frock and cowl, and be beaten in their shirt only… When they lie down in bed, let a master be among them with his rod and – if it be night – a candle, holding the rod in one hand and candle in the other… None doth ever speak to the other, except with the master's express permission, and in the hearing of all the others… Each boy must report whatever he knows against another; otherwise, if it is found that he deliberately concealed something, both will be beaten.* ❖

BECOMING A MERCHANT

Now that he is 16, the young man wants to become prosperous. He believes the way to do this is to buy and sell what people cannot do without. He sees that the goods that produce wealth for individuals in his town are either luxuries that well-off people need – French and Spanish wine, spices or expensive cloths and fabrics – or ordinary goods that are always needed, because they are consumed or they wear out, like clothes and shoes. He would like to be a merchant eventually but he decides that the way to start is with cheap, necessary goods, not luxuries.

Travelling merchants, or chapmen, went between towns on horseback.

whatever he can buy cheap in the town and sell in the village for a small profit.

He does well, and buys a pack-horse. He is robbed once, in the forest, and loses woollen cloths of various colours and a pack of shoes. He has to buy another supply of cloth and clothing goods and start on his travels again. He loads his horse up with shoes, purses, hats, chemises – shirts – some three-penny tunics for landless serfs, cloth for peasant

The chapman's life

The young man decides to try life as a chapman or pedlar, travelling the winding tracks between farms, villages and towns, selling at house-doors, markets and fairs. Off he goes on foot, the sack on his back stuffed with anything from ribbons, knives and decorated belts to shoes and herbal remedies:

It became common practice to share the cost and risks of exporting goods by sea. This extract is from a partnership document written in 1248 which records an agreement to share the cost and risk of hiring or buying or constructing ships to carry goods between Marseilles and Genoa:

❖ *I, James Lavagne, acknowledge to you, William Cadenet, citizen of Marseilles, that I have bought for you under your name, at Genoa, a sixth part in a certain ship which is called St Leonard, at a price of forty-one (Genoese) pounds and two solidi and six denarii in which Hugh Quillian and William Sansier are partners with me. And I bought a thirty-third part in a ship called the St Agnes, at a price of fifty (Genoese) pounds, in which ship Bonvassal Castel and his associates are partners.* ❖

tunics, best wool cloth, and a little silk cloth. He uses all the daylight he can, summer and winter. He does not dawdle in ale-houses. He has a cheery smile for the peasant-women in their gardens and a tickle under the chin for their toddlers. Villagers welcome him. After a year's successful travelling, he is confident about the future.

Expanding horizons
The young man buys another horse, and adds pans, pottery and gardening tools to his wares. Occasionally he even hires a boat to carry heavy goods like iron farming implements up rivers to sell in towns, and along the coast. He meets other traders at markets and fairs, and gets to know some real merchants.

He has almost saved enough money to set himself up as a merchant when he takes a great risk; he puts most of his savings in a ninth share of a ship travelling with wool, grain and fish to the great port of Bruges.

It pays off. No pirates raid the ship, no storms assail it and the vessel arrives safely in port.

Here the Journey of the Magi, *as painted by Bonozzo Gozzoli in the 1460s, is seen as a trading journey over a mountain pass with pack-horses and fantasy camels.*

MARRIAGE

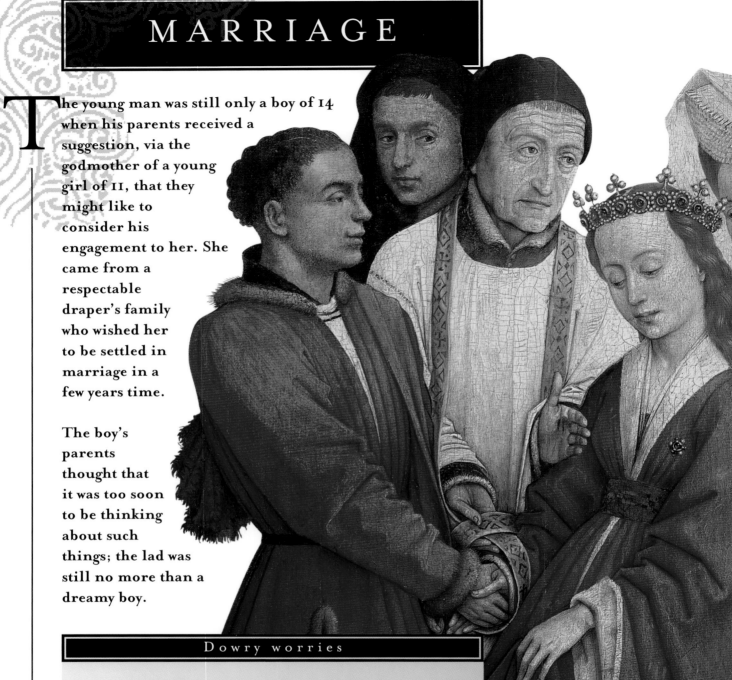

The young man was still only a boy of 14 when his parents received a suggestion, via the godmother of a young girl of 11, that they might like to consider his engagement to her. She came from a respectable draper's family who wished her to be settled in marriage in a few years time.

The boy's parents thought that it was too soon to be thinking about such things; the lad was still no more than a dreamy boy.

Dowry worries

Marriage arrangements relating to gifts and dowries had to satisfy both sets of parents. Here Margery Brews writes anxiously to John Paston III (1477) that her father will not give more than he has already promised:
❖ *My mother has worked hard with my father but she cannot get any more money than you know about, and, God knows, I am very sorry about it. But if you love me, as I hope you do, you will not leave me. For if you had only half the wealth you have, I would not leave you.* ❖

The wedding ceremony outside the church door, with the priest officiating.

Betrothal

Four years later, the matter is raised again. This time, it seems a good business idea for both families. The amount that the girl's father says he is willing to give her as a dowry to take into the marriage seems satisfactory. Now it will be wise to see if the 18-year-old boy and the 15-year-old girl are happy in each other's company.

The couple spend some time together and when it seems that they are well-suited, relatives and friends are gathered to hear the girl's father promise the young merchant-to-be her hand in marriage. The families' representatives shake hands on the contract, which includes details of the dowry she will bring to the marriage. The couple 'plight their troth' with a 'hand-fasting'.

A few weeks later, after the priest has called the banns three times in church, they attend the wedding ceremony at the church door. The bride is formally presented to her future father-in-law; the bridegroom places the ring on her finger. They enter the church for a Nuptial (wedding) Mass. The very same evening, the wedding banquet is held at the bride's parents' house.

Wedding

Special cooks have been hired and servants in uniforms. Large amounts of food appear, but the bride hardy touches the meal. At the end gifts are presented, music sounds, and a child is placed in the bride's lap, and a gold coin in her shoes: one the symbol of fertility, the other of riches.

Afterwards, a noisy procession follows the couple back to the house. There is singing, giggling, and a joke in poor taste: the bride is told that her husband of an hour has ridden away on his horse, scared at the whole idea of marriage to her!

A medieval party – wedding-guests dance to bagpipes and tabor.

THE WOOL TRADE

The successful married chapman has become a wool merchant, making expensive, lengthy and sometimes hazardous journeys to buy newly-sheared wool, transport it to a market, and sell it. He rides to the Cotswolds, Oxfordshire, where he believes the best wool is to be found. English wool, the most expensive, is the wool that Flemish and Italian cloth-makers want to make into the best quality cloth. There is cheaper wool to be had from the Italian hills, if he wished to travel there, or in Spain and North Africa.

The merchant shares a meal with his suppliers.

Buying in the Cotswolds

In the towns of Burford and Northleach he meets men who have tended sheep all their working lives. He has a business arrangement with two sheep-farmers from whom he buys the summer's clip of wool, and the autumn's Lammas-time crop of fells, the wool and skins of sheep slaughtered and salted down for winter meat.

Over a drink, this year's deal is done. The wool will be checked for quality, ensuring that nothing worthless is mixed with it – no hair or straw. Each huge sack is labelled and numbered and sealed, before being loaded on wagons, or in sarplers (half-sacks) on the backs of pack-horses for the slow journey to London, or to one of the small ports on the south coast. At the ports, the collectors of customs for the King enter on a roll the names of merchants shipping wool, the amounts and the quality.

The different activities of sheep farming, with shearing in the foreground.

Crossing the Channel

The ship that sails for Calais from one of the small south-coast ports is one of the smaller ships, a hundred tonnes. On board are about twenty sailors, men ready to keep off pirates with bows and arrows, cannon and gunpowder. The crossing might take three days. It might – if there are storms – take two weeks, or even more.

It is a great relief when journeys are accomplished safely in only a few days – with no pirates, no storms, no fires on board and nothing lost over the side.

The Staple at Calais

It was not always the case, but all English wool now comes to Calais, except smuggled wool, and the

wool bought by Italian merchants who can export direct to Italy by ship. It is at Calais - then owned by England - that the 14th century Staplers have their headquarters, the group of merchants who control the English wool trade.

In Calais the wool is checked again, one sample sack opened and the seal broken. The Staple must check that the wool is what the labels say it is; that none of the sacks have been tampered with, or re-labelled. Custom, in money, and subsidy, in wool, is then collected for the English monarch.

It is ready for sale. Flemish, German, Burgundian and Italian merchants are waiting. But they must change their coins into English money first. There is a mint at Calais, to make the English gold coins that non-English merchants will have to buy with their own coins before they buy wool. Only then can they carry it onwards, to the towns of the cloth-makers.

The merchant avoids time-consuming journeys if he can. His business is often better served by hard work in the office and counting house. Even so, the wool trade often takes him not only across the Channel to Calais, but sometimes further, to markets at Antwerp and Paris, to Avignon, over the Alps to the commercial towns of Italy, Florence, Venice and Genoa.

TRAVEL AND COMMUNICATION

Weeks and months of the merchant's life are spent travelling. And though the fastest messenger, changing horses, can do 160 kilometres in a day, a train of horses carrying goods averages no more than 25 or so. So, if he travels the length of France, it is a 20-day trip; crossing the Alps takes five to seven days; Paris to Naples, over the Alps, is a five-week journey.

Tolls and towns

Slow travel is made slower, and trading more expensive, by all the local tolls and taxes the merchant has to pay: river tolls, bridge tolls, tolls on setting up stalls, tolls on loading up ships. On great rivers, like the Seine and the Rhine, there are tolls every 8 or 10 kilometres. And sometimes the tolls are not legal, more a kind of robbery.

The merchant travels from town to town, very slowly by our standards, covering perhaps 40 to 50 kilometres a day. He passes through villages on the way but prefers to be inside town walls at night, and has to arrive before the gate shuts and the curfew bell tolls. Up the main street he rides, past shops with sign-boards and stakes reaching out to hit his head, guiding his horse round slaughtered animals, dung-heaps,

A traveller and his assistant arrive at a tavern, to be greeted by a glass of wine.

A traveller eats a meal at a comfortable tavern while the cook stirs a pot hanging over the fire. From a late–15th–century woodcut.

and holes in the road, fending off barking dogs to find his way down narrow alleyways towards the market square and the inn.

Inns

In the inns where the merchant passes the night there are nearly always several beds in a room. Only occasionally can he have a room to himself. Sometimes he has to share a bed with other travellers. When they arrive his servant asks about the cleanliness of the rooms, in particular whether there are bugs, fleas, rats or mice. Of course, he will be told there aren't any.

His horse will be fed and watered in the stables below.

He eats supper with the other guests in the single eating room, amongst the regulars spending an evening drinking, gambling, singing and telling tales. Next morning, breakfast is a little bread and beer or water, or cake soaked in wine. He pays the bill and remembers to ask the inn-keeper the way to the next town; there are no sign-posts to help him.

Medieval facts

Walking through medieval towns could be unpleasant. Medieval sanitation was primitive. Big houses might have cess-pits, but in England only London had any system of conveying waste away: by means of underground wooden pipes. A gutter – or 'kennel' – ran down the middle of the streets to carry water away. Travellers had to beware of chamber-pots being emptied from upstairs windows, with the cry, 'Gardy loo!' – from the French – *Gardez l'eau* – 'Look out for the water!'.

Medieval facts

This grim little story was related by a 13th-century Italian writer. A merchant arrived late at an inn. In the small dormitory there were two men to every bed – except for one, with only one occupant. Who was dead. The merchant, unaware of this, got in beside him, found himself short of room in the bed, and pushed out his bed-fellow, who fell out of bed. The merchant, seeing him lying there dead, believed he had killed him.

WAR AND PIRACY

Inns and tolls are irritating nuisances, but not usually hazardous. Apart from the risk of plague, the greatest problems for merchants are the almost non-stop wars and the risk of physical attack from pirate ships at sea and bands of brigands on land. Carrying goods on rough tracks through forests, over swampy marshland and mountains is arduous and risky. Robber-gangs roam everywhere, especially in times of war.

Pirates

Even in peaceful times, pirates scour the trading routes in the Channel, the North Sea and the Mediterranean. It is often wiser for ships to travel in small convoys, of six or seven together. Exports might be banned altogether, otherwise, for the sake of security. The merchant plans his trading journeys carefully.

Pirate danger

An Italian merchant's letter referred to the perilously pirate-infested stretch of sea between mainland Spain and Majorca:

❖ *The* [pirate] *galley from Peniscola is in these seas, and they say she is bound for Majorca. God sink her speedily. I have goods to send to Barcelona and Majorca and they cannot sail on account of her.* ❖

Under attack

A merchant galley sailing from Portofino to Pisa in Italy met two pirate ships at the mouth of the River Arno, but repelled them. The galley went on up-river, trumpets and bagpipes sounding, sailors in shirt-sleeves. A short distance from Pisa:

❖ *...by the order of Ser Jacopo, thief and traitor, we came under fire from bowmen hidden in houses and in thickets along the bank, shooting arrows and bombards.* ❖

Local people joined in, and the galley turned back.

War was disastrous for trade. Here two opposing armies wait while discussions take place.

Robbers

On land, bad roads and derelict bridges make travellers easier prey for robbers. Bridges regularly fall into disrepair, and when those responsible – often the lords of the manor – refuse to act, bridges fall into the river or are closed.

There are no signposts either; sometimes the only way of knowing where the twists and turns of a track are meant to take you is by noting the marks made on trees, branches and stones.

The worst enemy

War is the worst enemy of trade. War in these times, between nations and within them, is like an endemic disease that keeps breaking out here or there without warning. When it does, merchants can either call a halt to their business, or carry on in the hope that the armies will not cross their route or plunder their wares.

In wartime rulers also need money to pay and equip soldiers, to pay off ransoms, or conquerors. They can raise a tax or a loan. For English kings a tax on wool is the obvious remedy. Loans from rich Italian wool merchants will help, too. If they are reluctant to lend, their exports can be banned or permission to trade at all withdrawn. In wartime, any merchant established in a foreign city is at risk.

These hazards are real and dramatic. But there is always one other risk on the merchant's mind. Not so dramatic, but just as real, is the chance of being cheated – being sold old wool for new, or poor quality for best; or by being swindled trying to work out the complicated exchange-rates.

SECRETS OF SUCCESS

Merchants and traders needed accurate weights – one way of delivering what they promised.

The young merchant is prospering. The Cotswold sheep-farmers he buys his wool from are trustworthy and reliable, and they produce some of the best wool in England – which also means the best in Europe. Since he buys his wool from them every year, they also trust him.

The cloth merchants who buy wool from him – Italian, Flemish, French and German – also find him reliable. He means what he says in his letters; he delivers what he promises.

Keeping up-to-date

He has kept up-to-date with modern developments in commerce. He worked hard to master the intricate and difficult matter of working out the values of different currencies, but now does it much more quickly because he has learned to calculate using the new numerals from the Muslim world. The ease of using them means he does not have to resort to cloth and counters for working out exchange values or tolls or writing and checking bills.

He knows about the new approaches of some Italian bankers, who do more nowadays than simply change money. They take it and keep it safely on deposit for their clients. They transfer it for them to other banks. They are willing to pay money for someone on the strength of seeing his signature on a note, when the person who signed it is not present. He has even become a banker himself, in a modest way, lending to other traders, though not to rulers to help pay for wars. He

knows merchants who have been ruined by a king's failure to pay after losing a war.

Good sense and some luck

Other traits of character have helped him become successful. He has been cautious; he has insured all his cargoes and sent reliable servants with them. He has not expected huge profits on massive deals but a modest level of profit on his routine trading. He pays taxes and subsidies promptly. He

The successful merchant must have been a shrewd judge of people. The Italian merchant Datini lived in permanent fear not only of plague, war, banishment and political upheaval, but also of treacherous dealing. He gives this advice to a colleague:

❖ *You are young, but when you have lived as long as I have and traded with many people, you will know that man is a dangerous creature, and that there is danger in dealing with him.* ❖

has also learned some Italian, and can speak with the Italian traders and bankers who live in Southampton and London. His French is good enough to allow him to talk with French merchants, too.

He is prompt and scrupulous in his correspondence, and willing to pay a messenger or common carrier. Many letters need to be drafted out in rough first. It all takes time.

He takes no risks travelling, and always makes use of a guide in unknown territory, even on short journeys. So his success is partly down to skill and hard work. With all this, he has been fortunate so far. His trade has not been seriously impeded by war. He has missed the worst of the floods, and none of his ships has yet sunk.

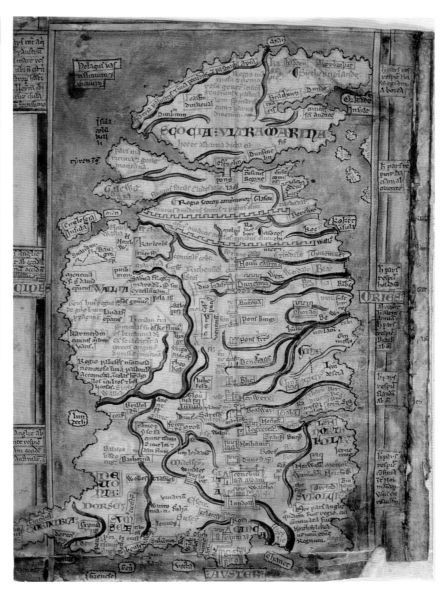

This medieval map of Britain shows how important rivers were, to the map-maker as to the merchant. Vague-looking by our standards, it was nonetheless very useful.

Medieval facts

Medieval merchants had to deal in a bewildering variety of currencies. They needed to know the value of coins as varied as the French crown, the Milan groat, the English florin and pound, the Burgundy rider, the Scottish guilder, the Florentine florin, the ducat of Venice — and more. There were small coins, like the denarius, or penny, whose value varied too, depending on how much valuable metal was used.

BRANCHING OUT

The years of travelling abroad to sell wool have taught the merchant many things. One is that making cloth may be more profitable than selling wool. He decides that he will use the wool he buys to make and sell cloth himself. This way he will avoid the expense, risk and sheer hard work involved in exporting wool. Wool is not selling as quickly as it once was; there is too much of it for sale, perhaps. In addition, there is a lighter export tax on cloth – 3 per cent rather than 25 per cent.

The Wife of Bath

One of the most memorable characters in Chaucer's *The Canterbury Tales* is 'The Wife of Bath'. She is a clothier, a manufacturer of woven cloth, and a very successful one:

❖ *Of clooth-makyng she hadde swich an haunt She passed hem of Ypre and of Gaunt.* ❖

The fact that her business is superior to those of Flanders, in Ypres and Ghent, suggests the importance of the English cloth industry.

Two women workers weave cloth.

Stages in cloth manufacturing

1 Shearing

4 Weaving

Cloth-making

Another factor affecting his decision is that cloth-making is well-established locally. There is water enough in the rivers and streams for those stages in the cloth-making that require it: the cleaning, dyeing and fulling, the last process now being done mechanically in riverside mills.

The other processes are established locally too: the carding and combing of tangled dirty wool, the spinning of it into yarn, the weaving of yarn into cloth, the dyeing of the cloth. Each trade has its established guild in the town. The merchant joins such a guild, that of the cloth-sellers.

As to whether local cloth-making can produce anything to rival beautiful Flemish tapestries, that is another matter: the main consideration is profit.

Shop

The merchant needs to open a shop. There he sells finished cloth,

as well as silks, velvet, tapestries, veils, tablecloths and napkins. He stocks other wares connected with fabrics and the implements needed to make things with them: thread, scissors, knives, hammers. He sells imported dyes: madder, woad, weld and the alum needed for the fabric to hold a dye.

His success gives him confidence. He opens a second shop, which sells goods imported from Spain, Africa and the Mediterranean: leather from Tunis and Cordoba, sword blades from Toledo, maps from Barcelona, ivory tusks and ostrich feathers and eggs from the Barbary Coast. His wares now are even more varied then the chapman's wares he once sold.

2 Carding

3 Spinning yarn

5 Dyeing

6 Fulling

WEALTH AND PROPERTY

Wealth and success have come to the merchant. His time is increasingly spent not in planning how to make money but in planning how to spend it. As well as shops, he possesses one or two small houses in addition to his own. He is wealthy enough to buy town properties as they come on the market.

His own recently purchased house, set in its own garden and orchard space a short distance from his main shop, is full of expensive hangings, pictures and beautiful furniture, a few pieces draped with Italian silks. Some of the most stunning wall-coverings, tapestries from Arras, are kept in chests, to be brought out on feast-days and special occasions.

Farming

The Italian merchant Datini bought a farm near Prato. In November 1407 he went there:

❖ *...to get the sowing done and the olives picked.* But he found that farming at a distance was not easy:

...I stayed there till nightfall without food or drink — I had to shout at the men about a number of things... Meo the foreman is not there, and I think nothing will get done unless I am there myself; the time for sowing is slipping by, and the olives are falling into ditches and getting carried away. ❖

A 15th-century view of a prosperous northern European town showing wealthy merchants' houses and a splendid walled garden in the foreground.

A meal by the fireside in the merchant's warm and welcoming farmhouse in winter.

Furnishings

In most rooms there are mirrors, and vases, jugs and bowls, including some silver ones. There is fine furniture — chairs, tables, chests, cupboards — all through the house. There is glass in the window-openings, and one bedroom has stained glass depicting a well-known story from a poem. The bedrooms have feather-beds, with canopies and foot-boards, and even small truckle-beds for the servants.

The house has been improved, also. Now there is an indoor privy (toilet). Chimneys have been built to channel smoke from the fires out of the house. The main fire in the hall burns coal.

The hall is the merchant family's main living space but there are stairs up to a gallery and upstairs rooms. The hall walls are painted with biblical scenes and episodes from poets' stories.

The merchant has paid for a tiled floor to be laid in the hall, rather than using rushes. There is one expensive carpet, usually draped over a table, as well as benches, stools, a screen, fire-irons and bellows around the fireplace.

A farm

The merchant has always liked the idea of having a farm in the country. He has bought pieces of land here and there, and is now negotiating to buy the large farmhouse he has seen, five or six kilometres outside the town. Going out there, making plans about orchards and vineyards, herb gardens and pasture, takes up more and more of his time.

MERCHANT'S WIFE

The merchant's wife no longer helps in the shop. Her work there is done by apprentices and journeymen assistants. She is also aware of her social position: wives of rich merchants do not help in the shop. But now she probably works even harder. She is in charge not only of an expanding household, including servants and children, but also, when her husband is away, of the business itself. She oversees his workers, deals with some of the correspondence and checks on the running of the shops.

Medieval facts

Evidence from medieval taxes suggests that, between the ages of 20 and 40, probably through the risks of childbirth, women's death-rate was higher than men's. After the age of 40, men's was higher than women's.

Seated in her comfortable home by a splendid roaring fire and dressed in expensive fabrics, the merchant's wife has good reason to be pleased with her husband's success.

Running the household

Running the house means buying food and drink and anything else that might be needed, from clothes to garden tools to wall hangings and pictures. It means supervising all the daily household work, from basic cleaning and washing, to sewing and embroidery. The merchant's wife does some weaving herself, and checks that the brewing and candle-making is done properly.

She supervises the servants she has hired, going round the large house checking on their work. She is in and out of the kitchen all day long: cooks need watching.

Books of advice

The long day leaves her little time for reading one of the books in which writers advise the wives of merchants how to run a household economically and efficiently. The books suggest that wives should train servants, buy and budget sensibly, and make sure that the house is so pleasant that the husband will always want to bring his friends home. Then, at the end of his life, these writers say with a knowing wink, he will be aware of how much she has done for him, and leave his house and household goods to her in his will.

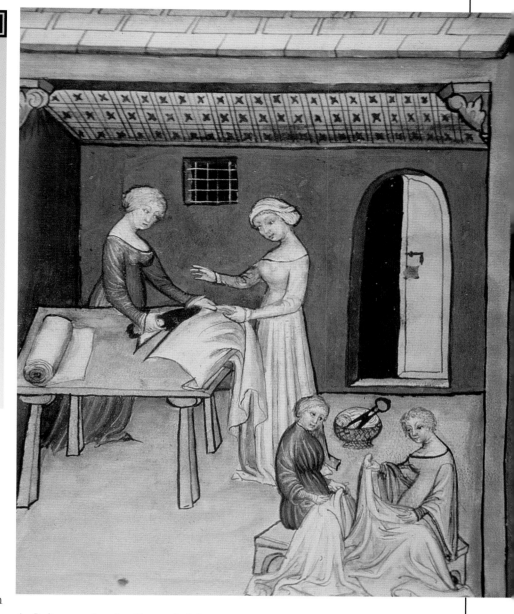

The good wife

A merchant in 14th-century Paris, France, wrote a book for his much younger wife, advising and instructing her about how she should be a good wife to him, and to the young man she would marry after his death! He wrote that when she goes out to church or into the town, it should be with her duenna or maid, and she should behave modestly:

❖ *...walking with head up, eyes lowered and quiet and looking straight in front of you on the ground, looking at neither man nor woman and stopping to speak to no-one in the street.* ❖

And she hardly needs them to remind her that she should go early to Mass, say her prayers quietly, and share meat and wine with the poor. Or that she should also know how to get rid of fleas, clean heavy, fur-trimmed garments, and keep the weeds from the garden and make sure there are no holes in the fence for children to creep in and steal the fruit.

An Italian merchant's wife cuts cloth for a customer.

And the children

As if that were not enough, there have always been the children. They have been brought up carefully, in her care, though servants have helped, looking out for them and accompanying them into town sometimes. But the mother has had the responsibility for seeing to their food and clothing, for beginning to teach them how to read and write, and instructing them in religious matters, ensuring they learn their prayers and say them.

With her husband she has arranged for their son's schooling and chosen women who come to the house to teach their daughter. It has been her aim above all to have the children brought up to be disciplined and well-behaved, their son to be courteous, their daughter to be kind and modest.

The merchant's wife is a very busy woman.

GOOD WORKS

Medieval facts

A wealthy Bath clothier, William Phillips, founded the Hospital of St Catherine and completely restored St Catherine's Chapel in St Mary's Church. St Catherine was the patron saint of spinning – an ideal guardian for a cloth town.

—◆—

The merchant has always been aware that in theory the Church looks down on profit-making: even though it makes money itself in all kinds of ways. He knows Saint Jerome's famous saying: *Homo mercator vix aut nunquam potest Deo placere* [*The merchant can seldom or ever please God*]. He must please God in other ways. And he is determined to please God, to be sure after death of his place in Heaven.

Nobles and a bishop distribute charity to the needy, including (left) a man on crutches and (right) a pilgrim.

The after-life

He thinks a great deal these days about the after-life, for which, as the Church teaches and he believes, this life on earth is only a brief time of preparation. There is a well-known saying that he repeats grimly to himself: *Salvandorum paucitas, damnandorum multitudo* – [Few are saved; many damned].

The least he can do to help his soul is to go on a pilgrimage. Merchants he knows have been to Canterbury, Rome, Jerusalem and Spain, to the shrine of St James at Santiago de Compostela. He chooses to do penance by travelling to Compostela. His wife will take care of his business affairs.

The account-books of the Italian merchant Datini record frequent payments of alms, or charitable gifts. Here is one entry:

❖ *March 27, 1395. 1 lira… to give, for the love of God, to a poor woman whose son is in prison and will shortly need to have his leg cut off.* ❖

His charity emerges in letters too, like this to his wife:

❖ *I hope to send you a bale of herrings and about a thousand oranges. You must sell half the oranges and give the other half to whomever you please. And the same with the herrings, or, if you please, give away all the herrings and oranges, the greater part to God in alms, the rest to kinsfolk and friends, rich and poor.* ❖

A close friend praised his charitable practices:

❖ *I think there are more than twenty-five families now alive thanks to you — and God. You give help to more than a hundred a year.* ❖

A group of pilgrims sets out.

Pilgrimage to Spain

In April, he finally dons the pilgrim's robe, takes the pouch with thread and sewing needle, the coins of gold and silver, the staff and the sober hat. For all pilgrims they symbolise the bindingness of charity, the sharpness of penance; then silver for grace, gold for glory, the staff for the wood of the Cross, the cloak for His humanity and the hat for the Crown of Thorns. They journey 'in Christ'. He knows the roads well enough, and the inns. The group he travels with is from all sections of society, except the poor, who always seem to have to work. He returns feeling that a place in Heaven may be his. The long, long journey leaves him tired, but fulfilled.

In the following year, when he is less strong, he pays a priest to go to Rome, the centre of the Roman Catholic Church, to stay there for a year, praying for his soul.

Endowments

The merchant wishes also to be remembered more publicly in the town, as a religious man. He gives money to various churches in the region, and a great deal to his own church. He pays for roof repairs and to make the church bigger. It is agreed he will be buried there, and his descendants. The charity is sincere but it is also what most merchants do. Charity is considered to be not only spiritually good for the giver, but to strengthen claims to the reward of an after-life in Heaven.

HEALTH AND DIET

The merchant's father and mother, and one of his children, died in the first and most terrible of the waves of plague that have swept along the trade-routes of Europe. Dread of plague fills everyone's mind. Everyone believes that religion and health are the best defences against it.

An apothecary weighs out the ingredients of a remedy for one of his customers.

Diet

Eating and drinking healthily have always been important considerations in the merchant's family, but become more so as he ages. The merchant talks and writes a good deal about his health and about food. He eats just two meals a day, usually skipping breakfast, except for sometimes the luxury of a little bread and water, or – to keep away the plague – wine. Dinner, the first meal, is at about 10 in the morning, after an hour or two at work, and supper at sunset.

He has been lucky in many ways. No broken bone has needed setting. No bladder stone has needed removal, or cataract in the eye. He has had teeth taken out, painfully, when his remedy for toothache didn't work.

Plague myths

The causes of plague were not known. For many, it was a punishment from Heaven for wrong-doing. As the English poet William Langland, in *Piers Plowman*, puts it:

❖ *These pestilences were for pure sin.* ❖

Acute fear of plague produced religious hallucinations, as in Messina, in southern Italy, where:

❖ *A black dog with a drawn sword in his paws appeared among them, gnashing his teeth and rushing upon them and breaking all the silver vessels and lamps and candlesticks on the altars and throwing them hither and thither...* ❖

Advice to surgeons

In a book of advice and hints to practitioners about surgical operations, a famous 14th century English doctor emphasised the importance of the positions of the stars and planets:

❖ *But most important of all is that he do not operate at any time when operation is forbidden by the astronomers.* ❖

Gathering fruit for medicinal use.

The doctor

His doctor checks his pulse and his urine regularly. Occasionally, during times when he has caught an infection or become exhausted, he has been prescribed treatments such as *aurum potabile* – drinkable gold cordial – and pills of powdered stag's horn or emerald. He distrusts these expensive remedies though, believing doctors prescribe them only to rich clients.

His doctor's main recommendations for staying healthy are to do with diet and exercise. It is wise to take a little exercise before meals; have a block of wood and a saw handy. It is wise to wait for two hours after eating before going to bed. Avoid rich foods. On no account eat pies.

Avoiding stress

Peace and quiet are also essential to health, say the doctors. The merchant should take care not to be upset by barking dogs or noisy neighbours. It is also bad for the health to take matters too much to heart and feel angry, though an occasional burst of fury and shouting is a healthy release.

His health, though, despite good advice and the care of his wife, is less good than it was. He is ill from time to time. He needs a stick to walk with, and eye-glasses to read.

Distrust of doctors

In 1464 Margaret Paston expressed her mistrust of doctors in a letter to her husband:
❖ *For God's sake beware of any medicine you get from any physician in London. I shall never trust them because of what happened to your father and uncle.* ❖

But she does believe in 'treacle of Genoa'. This is from a letter to him in 1451:
❖ *I ask you heartily that you quickly send me a pot of treacle. For I have been very worried, and your daughter too, since you went away. One of the tallest young men in the parish lies sick and has a great fever.* ❖

The travelling doctor loses no time checking a patient's urine.

Medieval facts

Because the cause of the plague was a mystery, wild beliefs abounded about it. In Lithuania a 'Pest Maiden' was thought to wave a red scarf at the door of a house, so as to infect it. One man waited for the Pest Maiden at his door and when she reached in to wave the scarf he chopped off her arm. He died, but saved the village. The scarf was preserved in the church as a holy relic.

THE END

The merchant has died on his farm, wandering in the vineyard there. On his last journey home to his house in the town, laid on a bier in a cart hauled by old pack-horses, he is accompanied by a priest; and six poor men carrying candles walk on each side.

❖ *20 marks to hire one chaplain to go on pilgrimage to Rome and to remain there throughout one year, to celebrate and pray for my soul and the souls for whom I am bound to pray, and £10 to hire two men to go on pilgrimage for my soul to St James in Galicia.* ❖

'St James in Galicia' refers to Santiago de Compostela, Spain.

The wake

For the wake, held in the church where his body lies, the hearse is draped in black cloth. Round it sit 20 or so priests, as well as learned clerics and choristers, and about 60 poor men and women. They are all singing from their psalters, chanting prayers for the dead merchant's soul.

A great crowd of people is needed. Their prayers are needed, to support his soul and speak up to Heaven for it, as evidence of the merchant's goodness. All who are there will receive a gift.

All members of the guild are expected at the wake. There are regulations to ensure it is observed properly. In his will he has

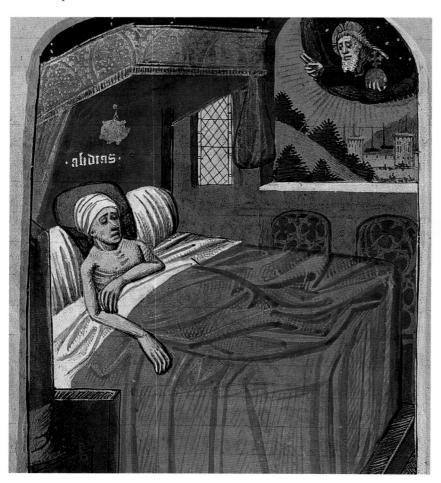

The merchant lies on his lonely death-bed as God calls him to Heaven.

Bequests

John Burghard from Lynn, England, gives detailed instructions for many bequests and gifts of money, especially for the upkeep of churches and — as befits a merchant — roads and bridges. He gives:

❖ *Towards the fabric of the chapel of St Nicholas, 10s... [as well as] ...towards the fabric of 6 other local churches. [He leaves] ...20s towards the repair of Setchey causeway and money for repairs also to Stoke bridge.* ❖

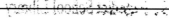

A wealthy merchant's funeral is a solemn but grand affair.

wine for 'the quality', or important people and beer for the rest. Seventy servers look after them all.

The merchant leaves his house, lands and property to his widow. He details all the particular objects that will be hers: beds, silver, cloths and tapestries; carts and cattle; and so on.

He is rich enough to leave money for the repair of the church roof; for the carving of a ship in the nave of the church, and for a priest to sing prayers daily for his soul for ten years. There are money-gifts for various people he has worked with, including his old farmer-friends in the Cotswolds, whose good wool he bought for so long.

He asks that a tomb be built, with a likeness of himself, on a carved stone bust, above it. He is – was – determined not to be forgotten.

emphasised there should be no masks or mockery. He also asks that no-one but his wife should be clothed in black.

The funeral services themselves are grand and solemn. Vespers, or evensong, is held on the evening before the funeral, Matins early the next morning, then the Mass for the Dead. Then he is buried in the churchyard, to the ringing of the bells of his own church and two others nearby.

The feast and the will

At the feast that follows there is an abundance of food and drink: beef and pork, goose and fish. There is

GLOSSARY

Arras ❖ a kind of luxurious tapestry made at Arras, in Artois

Artisan ❖ a craftsman or woman, such as an embroiderer or blacksmith

Banns ❖ the priest 'calls the banns' for a prospective couple three times, asking in church whether anyone objects to the marriage

Betrothal ❖ being engaged to marry

Burgess ❖ a wealthy and respectable inhabitant of a town

Chapman ❖ from 'cheap', meaning bargain or haggle: a small-scale seller of articles of various sorts, usually a traveller

Cordwainer ❖ a dealer in leather from (through mispronunciation) Cordoba, in Spain

Confession ❖ the private admission of sins to a priest

Crusader ❖ a person (usually a knight) who went off to fight in one of the many 'holy wars' against Muslims in the Middle East during the medieval period

Dowry ❖ the money and goods a father gave his daughter when she married

Endowment ❖ a gift of money usually to a religious or educational foundation

Fair ❖ lords were 'granted' fairs to allow the sale of goods of all kinds in one place

Feudalism ❖ the system of holding land in return for agreed services or 'works'

Fulling ❖ hammering the finished cloth to smoothe it, an increasingly mechanised process in late-medieval times

Grammar ❖ rules of a language

Guild ❖ an organisation of members of a certain craft, with rules for working, and for the production and sale of materials; also called a 'mystery'

Hand-fasting ❖ clasping of the hands in betrothal

Herbal ❖ a book of medicinal herbs, with diagrams

Mass ❖ the central religious service of the Church, enacting the ceremonial consumption of bread and wine, 'the body and blood of Christ'; sung by the priest in Latin

Midden ❖ a rubbish heap

Mystery play ❖ a biblical story acted out by members of a craft or mystery

Payment in kind ❖ payment with articles of produce, eg eggs

Plighting troth ❖ making a promise to marry

Primer ❖ a small handwritten manuscript with extracts for children to learn to read from

Sack ❖ a measured quantity of wool, such that a cart was needed to transport it

Sarpler ❖ a quantity of wool, about half the amount of a 'sack'

Serf ❖ a 'servile' or unfree person 'tied' or 'bound' to land they hold from a lord; a 'bondsman' or 'villein'

Shop ❖ usually a house with the downstairs used for trading, selling through the 'window' at the front

Staple ❖ an arrangement for buying and selling at particular places, usually towns, making the collection of customs easier and more reliable

Subsidy ❖ a tax in kind; so, on wool, a certain amount of wool

Wake ❖ the ceremony of 'watching', overnight, the dead person's body

Yarn ❖ wool when spun into strands

TIMELINE

c. 1000 onwards for c 200 years – great expansion of population across Europe
1066 William of Normandy invades England – in December, crowned King
1088 Papacy split – two competing popes
c. 1090 guild of weavers at Mainz
1096 First Crusade begins
1107 trade guild set up in Burford, Oxfordshire – perhaps the first in England
1135–1154 civil war in England
1146–1254 further crusades – 2nd to 7th
c. 1150 importation of silk culture to Sicily
c. 1150 on – European rulers grant cities rights to hold regular markets and fairs
c. 1190 first windmills in Europe
c. 1200 onwards – money rents replacing labour services across Europe – growth of towns, trade and money economy – increase in supply of coins - demand for luxury goods
c. 1200 onwards – growth of banking system in cities of north and central Italy – trading communities of foreign merchants in Europe and Middle East
1208 King John quarrels with Pope - Pope bans church services in England
1209 founding of Cambridge University
1214 barons demand charter of liberties from John
1265 Marco Polo travels to Far East
1275 First customs duty on export of wool and leather
1279 new silver coins in England – groat [4d], round farthing and halfpenny
1285 spectacles made in northern Italy
1291 Genoese vessels try to sail round Africa
1294 Edward takes control of English wool trade
1317 heavy rains and ruined harvests – famine across Europe
1323–28 peasant revolts in Netherlands
1337 outbreak of Hundred Years War between England and France
1344 first English gold coin – noble, worth 6s 8d
1346 Calais (then English) established as 'staple' town for English wool trade – all wool had to pass through it
1348-1349 arrival of bubonic plague, 'Black Death', in Europe
c. 1350 first marine insurance contracts
1357 long-distance courier service set up by 17 Florentine companies
c. 1360–1400 fall in export of English wool
1361 further episode of plague
1369 harvests fail across Europe
1381 Peasants' Revolt in England
1437–38 ruined harvests famine and plague in many parts of Europe
1438–40 heavy rains and ruined harvests in England
c. 1450 invention of printing with moveable type
1450 French defeat the last English army to be sent to Normandy
1450–1471 The Wars of the Roses in Britain
1498 Vasco da Gama lands at Calicut, India

INDEX

A

after-life 36, 37
apothecary 38
apprentices 12, 16, 34, 41
artisans 9, 12, 42

B

banking 9, 28, 29
banns, wedding 21, 42
baptism 10
bequests 40, 41
betrothal 21
Black Death 8, 27
books, advice 34, 35, 38
burgesses 9, 18, 42
burial 41

C

Calais 23
calculations 12, 17, 28
Canterbury Tales, The 9, 30
chapman 9, 18-19, 22, 31, 42
charity 36, 37
Chaucer, Geoffrey 9, 30
childbirth 10, 11, 34
childhood 10-17
children 10-17, 34, 35, 38
church 9, 10, 11, 13, 20, 21, 35, 37, 39, 40, 41, 42
Church 10, 11, 36, 42
churching 11
cloth, wool 18, 19, 22, 30-31
    silk 19, 31, 32
clothes 9, 10, 12, 14, 18, 21, 34
clothier 22, 23, 30-31, 36
cloth-making 30-31
Cotswolds 22, 28, 41
crusades 8, 42
currencies, foreign 23, 28, 29
customs 22

D

doctors 39
dowry 20, 21, 42
drapers 20, 31, 41

E

education 16-17, 35
endowments 37, 42
entertainment 14, 15, 35

F

fair 14, 18, 19, 42
farming 8, 9, 32, 33
    sheep 22, 23, 28
festivals 15
feudalism 8, 9
Flanders 9, 22, 28, 30, 31
funeral 41
furniture 11, 12, 32, 33

G

games 14, 15
gifts, charitable 36, 37
guilds 12, 14, 31, 40, 42

H

hand-fasting 21, 42
houses 12-13
Hundred Years War 8, 27

I/J/K

inns 25, 26, 37, 38
Italy 9, 21, 22, 23, 25, 26, 27, 28, 29, 31, 32, 35, 37, 38
journeymen 34
kings 8, 10, 22, 27, 28

L

Langland, William 38
lords 8, 21, 24, 27, 42

M

manors 8, 21, 27
markets 9, 13, 14, 18, 19, 22, 23, 25
marriage 20-21, 42
Mass 21, 35, 41, 42
merchant,
    death of 40-41
    diet of 11, 25, 38-39
    health of 38-39, 40
    housing of 12-13, 32-33
    lifespan of 34
    marriage of 20-21
    wife of 10-11, 12, 34-35, 41
monks 16, 17
mortality, child 10, 38

P

pack-horses 13, 18, 19, 22, 40
peasants 8, 9, 18, 19

pedlars 18-19
pilgrimage 36, 37, 40
pirates 19, 23, 26-27
plague 8, 10, 21, 26, 27, 29, 38, 39
priests 10, 20, 21, 23, 37, 40, 41, 42
privy 13, 33
punishments 17

R

refuse 13
remedies 11, 18, 38, 39
robbers 18, 24, 27
routes, trade 22, 23, 26, 28, 29, 38

S

sanitation 13, 25
Santiago de Compostela 36, 40
school 16-17
service, work 8, 9, 42
ships, merchant 19, 23, 24, 26, 27, 29
shopkeepers 9, 12, 16
shops 10, 12, 13, 14, 31, 32, 34
sport 14, 15
Staple, the 22, 23

T

tavern 13, 24, 25
taxes 24, 27, 28, 30, 34, 42
tolls 24, 26, 28, 42
towns 8, 9, 12-13, 14, 16, 18, 19, 22, 24, 25, 35, 36, 37, 40
trade, wool 22-23
travel 8, 18, 19, 22-25

W

wake 40, 42
war 8, 10, 26, 27, 28, 29
weaving 9, 30, 31, 34
wedding 20, 21
wills 12, 34, 40, 41

These are the lists of contents for each title in *Medieval Lives*:

Peasant

Introduction · First years · Peasant cottage · Childhood
The Church · Marriage · Land · Work-service for the manor · The manorial court
The working year · Feeding the family · Sickness and health · Women's work · Earning money
Games and entertainment · Freedom · Last days · Glossary · Timeline/Useful websites · Index

Merchant

Introduction · First days · House and home · Growing up · School · Becoming a merchant
Marriage · The wool trade · Travel and communication · War and piracy · Secrets of success
Branching out · Wealth and property · The merchant's wife · Good works · Health and diet
The end · Glossary · Timeline/Useful websites · Index

Knight

All about knights · A future knight is born · Time to leave home · Becoming a squire
A squire goes forth · Becoming a knight · Invitation to the castle · Joust! · Called to war
Battlefield tactics · Dressed to kill · Weapons · Siege warfare · Pilgrimage · Returning home
Knightly duties · Death of a knight · Glossary · Timeline/Useful websites · Index

Nun

Introduction · Birth · Childhood and education · To the nunnery — postulant
The nunnery itself · Taking the veil — novice · Daily life — the offices · The inner life
Daily routine · Enclosure · Cellaress and librarian · The world outside · Priests and nuns
Poverty and personal possessions · A visitation · Difficult times · Death · Glossary
Timeline/Useful websites · Index

Lady of the Manor

A medieval lady · A lady is born · Invitation to a wedding
At home with a lady · Wifely duties · Noble children · A year in the life
Clothes and hairstyles · A lady's hobbies · A lady's books · Time to eat · The lady falls ill
Women who work · The noblest ladies · A visit to a nunnery · The world outside
Widowhood · Glossary · Timeline/Useful websites · Index

Stonemason

Introduction · Birth · Childhood and growing up · Training - the quarry
Training - the building site · Rough-mason — a bridge · Summoned to work - a castle
A real 'mason' - the abbey · A growing reputation · Stone-carver · The lodge
Under-mason for the college · Master-mason for the cathedral · Designing the cathedral
Building the cathedral · Retirement · End of a life · Glossary · Timeline/Useful websites · Index